EXTREME SUMMER
SPORTS ZONE

BMX VERT

Patrick G. Cain

Lerner Publications Company • Minneapolis

Lerner Publications Company
A division of Lerner Publishing Group, Inc.
241 First Avenue North
Minneapolis, MN 55401 U.S.A.

Website address: www.lernerbooks.com

Content Consultant: Cody York, professional BMX photographer

Library of Congress Cataloging-in-Publication Data

Cain, Patrick G.
     BMX vert / by Patrick G. Cain.
          p.   cm. — (Extreme summer sports zone)
     Includes index.
     ISBN 978–1–4677–0750–3 (lib. bdg. : alk. paper)
     1. Bicycle motocross—Juvenile literature. I. Title.
GV1049.3.C35 2013
796.6'22—dc23   2012033888

Manufactured in the United States of America
1 – BP – 12/31/12

Photo credits: The images in this book are used with the permission of: Backgrounds: © Jeff Gross/ Getty Images, 4-5; © Cody York/www.codyyorkphotography.com, 6, 11, 12, 15, 17, 18, 19, 20, 21, 25, 26, 28, 29; © Sue McDonald/Shutterstock Images, 7; © ISC Images & Archives/Getty Images, 8; © Getty Images, 9; © Everett Collection, 10; © SGranitz/WireImage/Getty Images, 13; © George Olsson/iStockphoto, 14, 27; © Harry How/Getty Images, 16; © Ben Haslam/Haslam Photography/ Shutterstock Images, 22, 24; © Andy Kropa/Getty Images, 23

Front cover: © Jeff Gross/Getty Images; © RTimages/Shutterstock.com (background).

Main body text set in Folio Std Light 11/17.
Typeface provided by Adobe Systems.

TABLE OF CONTENTS

CHAPTER ONE

WHAT IS BMX VERT?

It was the night of the 2012 X Games BMX vert (vertical) competition, and vert rider Jamie Bestwick was ready to make history. Bestwick was a legend in the BMX world. He had won the gold medal in the X Games vert competition every year since 2007. But Bestwick was 40 years old. That was unusually old for an action-sports star. He was the oldest vert competitor in the finals. He hadn't even won his qualifying heat. He came in second to rider Simon Tabron. Everyone wondered if Bestwick would be able to keep up his medal run.

THE X GAMES

ESPN has hosted an extreme sports competition known as the X Games every year since 1995. BMX vert was featured in the original competition. It has been a part of the Summer X Games ever since. Like in the Olympic Games, X Games athletes compete for gold, silver, and bronze medals. X Games athletes also win prize money. Most fans see the X Games as the most important action sports event of the year. Many vert competitors work for months trying to perfect a trick or a run. Because of this, many new tricks are performed at the X Games every year.

Jamie Bestwick took a big chance when he decided to become a professional vert rider. Bestwick was born and raised in England. Eventually he got a job working for a British company that repaired airplane engines. But Bestwick had always loved bikes. And he was great at riding them. He decided to quit his job. He then moved to the United States to try to become a pro BMX vert rider. This was a risky move. Fortunately it was the right one. He started competing in 1992 and never looked back. From 2000 to 2012, Bestwick won nine gold medals in the BMX vert X Games competition.

Bestwick won the first gold medal of this six-peat in 2007.

It was no contest. Bestwick dominated from the moment he first sped down the half-pipe ramp. Bestwick caught air (jumped vertically) 3 to 4 feet (0.9 to 1.2 meters) higher than the other vert riders. His tricks were hard. His runs were smooth. He even performed a new trick: a downside tailwhip to turndown. The judges were impressed. Bestwick's hard work had paid off. He won the gold medal. The win made him the first BMX vert rider to six-peat (win six times in a row) at the X Games. Bestwick had made history.

Bestwick's 2012 gold medal run captured what fans around the world love about BMX vert. Vert uses half-pipe ramps from 15 to 27 feet (4.6 to 8.2 m) high. Riders speed down and up these ramps.

They catch air (get airborne) and create awesome tricks. They put these tricks together to invent incredible runs. But no run is the same. Every vert rider is different. Each run reflects the rider's personality.

Being a BMX vert rider means getting back up after falling off a bike. Professional riders make tricks look easy. But each trick takes much practice. A lot of practice means a lot of falls. BMX vert riding can be very dangerous, so riders take safety seriously. They know a bad fall could mean a bad injury, which can end a rider's vert career.

Fans admire vert riders for more than just their bike skills. Riders such as Bestwick show fans they can do anything if they try hard and practice a lot. This dedication has helped make BMX vert a popular sport around the world. And the vert storm doesn't appear to be dying down anytime soon!

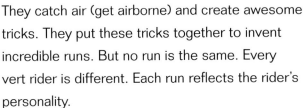
BMX vert riders, like this girl, use jumps to catch air.

7

BMX VERT BEGINS

BMX riders ruled streets across the United States long before ESPN held its first X Games in 1995. But before BMX made it to the streets, BMX riders were taking their bikes on off-road courses. In the 1960s, motocross was becoming a popular sport in California. At that time, most motocross riders raced motorbikes around dirt tracks. But not everyone could afford an expensive motorcycle. Soon kids started taking their road bicycles on these same courses. They used

In the 1960s and the 1970s, motocross riders raced motorcycles around dirt tracks.

The Schwinn Sting-Ray was the earliest version of a BMX bike.

the courses' jumps to catch air and do other tricks. This new sport was called bicycle motocross, shortened to BMX. A new bike released in 1963 helped make this new sport possible.

A New Kind of Riding

A new bike called the Schwinn Sting-Ray helped lead the bicycle revolution. By 1968 nearly 70 percent of all bikes sold in the United States were Sting-Rays or other bike companies' versions of it. The bike was sturdy. It could handle the sharp turns and small jumps of the motocross courses.

YAMAHA PRESENTS

ON ANY SUNDAY

THE MOST EXCITING FILM EVER MADE ON MOTORCYCLE SPORT
BY BRUCE BROWN, PRODUCER OF THE ENDLESS SUMMER

Although its subject was motorcycle racing, the documentary On Any Sunday introduced BMX bike riding to kids across the country.

BMX was becoming more popular. But it was still mostly confined to Southern California. However, a new film about motorcycle racing would change all that. In 1971 the documentary *On Any Sunday* was released. The documentary followed the sport of motorcycle racing. It featured major motorcycle stars of the time. One scene from the film showed kids on bicycles copying motorcycle moves on dirt tracks.

People across the country saw the movie and the bicycle scene. The movie gave BMX biking the exposure it needed. Soon kids across the United States were riding their bikes like kids in Southern California had been for years. Before long, kids started taking their bikes off the dirt courses. They practiced tricks in the streets. They used the walls of empty swimming pools as ramps to create tricks. The BMX bike was here to stay.

By the 1980s, the sport was changing. A new style of BMX called freestyle was becoming popular. Instead of racing, freestyle riders focused on doing tricks. These BMX riders sometimes practiced in skate parks. This meant that skateboarders and BMX riders were practicing together. Skaters learned from BMX riders. And the BMX riders learned from skaters.

Vert riders began using empty swimming pools to catch big air.

By 1983 BMXers could compete in events just for freestyle riders. Rider Bob Haro created a bike frame especially designed for freestyle riding. Haro's frame was extra sturdy. The new design could handle the ramps that freestyle riders were starting to use for tricks. In 1984 Ron Wilkerson took his feet off the bike pedals while airborne. The move was the first no-footed aerial. The trick opened the door to more BMX stunts, and riders started doing more difficult moves. They put tricks together to create combinations (known as combos).

Some contests started featuring events that used ramps. Riders could get big air on a half or quarter pipe. The ramps gave skilled riders a chance to defy gravity and push the limits. In 1989, 17-year-old rider Mat Hoffman used a half-pipe ramp to pull off

Half-pipe ramps allowed vert riders to try bigger tricks than ever before.

THE HISTORY OF THE HALF PIPE

In 1975 a teen skateboarder in California changed action sports forever. Tom Stewart and his friends had been skating in giant water pipes in the Arizona desert. The pipes were great for building speed and doing jumps. Tom decided to try to re-create the pipes in California. With the help of his older brother, Tom built a wooden half-pipe ramp in his yard. The design was almost immediately popular. Tom started his own company, Rampage, to sell the ramp. Soon the half pipe became an important part of many action sports, including BMX vert, in-line skating, snowboarding, and more.

the first 900. He sped up the ramp and rotated two and a half times before landing. Fans were stunned.

In 1991 Hoffman started his own bike company, Hoffman Bikes. He also hosted the first Bicycle Stunt Series competition in 1992. One of the events in his competition featured a ramp. Vert competitions were becoming more popular. Just three years later, ESPN held its first X Games competition, known at the time as Extreme Games. The X Games featured a vert-riding category.

Mat Hoffman helped make vert a popular category of BMX riding.

Modern BMX bikes are built to handle the tough tricks of a vert ramp.

By the late 1990s, bikes were starting to change. Riders took off their brakes and started riding with pegs. These changes allowed riders to pull off even more extreme moves on the vert ramp.

The tricks kept getting bigger. In 2001 Hoffman made history when he caught more than 50 feet (15 m) of air. He cleared 26.5 feet (8.1 m) above a 24-foot (7.3 m) quarter pipe. The trick created a new world record. Other riders like Jamie Bestwick, Chad Kagy, and Simon Tabron continued creating new tricks and pushing the limits of the sport. Vert riding was as exciting as ever.

Pro BMX vert rider Simon Tabron does a tucked no-hander.

SIMON TABRON

Simon Tabron turned pro in 1990. He has been one of the top vert riders ever since. He is a fierce competitor. Fans know him best for his ability to perform spinning tricks. He's participated in nearly every X Games since 1998. He won the Vert World Championship in 2002, 2003, and 2004. In 2012 he walked away with a bronze medal.

CHAPTER THREE

THE GEAR AND THE STUNTS

BMX bikes are pretty handy. Young riders can use their BMX bikes to ride to school or a friend's house. BMX pros use their bikes to do incredible stunts in a vert competition.

While the bike itself is important, safety gear is even more important. BMX vert is a dangerous sport. Top riders almost always practice with safety gear. Pros know that if they get injured, they likely won't be able to compete. If a rider can't compete, he or she can't make money. The X Games require vert riders to wear helmets while competing. Many riders wear other kinds of safety gear as well. Not wearing safety gear can be very dangerous.

Even pros such as Vince Byron take spills while competing in BMX vert.

BMX vert can be a dangerous sport. Pros like Chad Kagy stay safe by wearing the right safety gear.

The pros recommend a few must-haves for vert riders:

Helmets: Most BMX vert riders wear helmets made of hard plastic. Pro riders often wear full-face helmets. These helmets are often decorated with different patterns and graphics.

Knee pads: It's easy for a rider's feet to slip off the pedals during a jump. Knee pads protect a rider's knees from hitting the bike or the hard vert ramp during a fall.

Elbow pads: Most BMX riders also wear elbow pads. These guard a rider's elbows during spills.

BMX gloves: Many riders choose to wear BMX gloves. These help the rider keep a strong grip on his or her handlebars when going off the ramp. Gloves also protect a rider's hands during falls.

The Moves

When a new vert rider is getting started, it's important for that rider to practice tricks within his or her skill level. With enough practice, a rider may be able to try more advanced tricks. Vert riders often watch one another's tricks to learn new ones. But the best scores in competitions usually come when a rider does something new. Creativity is a huge part of vert. But all pros start somewhere. All pros learn a few basic tricks before they move on to the really innovative stunts.

One-Footer

To do a one-footer, the rider kicks his or her foot out to the side when catching air off the vert ramp. The rider puts that foot back on the pedal before landing.

Jay Eggleston does a one-footer at the 2008 X Games.

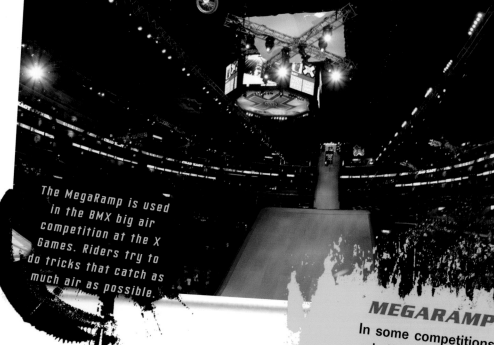

The MegaRamp is used in the BMX big air competition at the X Games. Riders try to do tricks that catch as much air as possible.

No-Hander

A no-hander is one of the most basic BMX vert tricks. A lot of pros use no-handers in combos with other tricks to earn a higher score during competitions. To do no-handers, riders take their hands off their handlebars while airborne. They pinch the seat between their knees to keep control of the bike. The rider's hands should be back on the handlebars before landing.

MEGARAMP

In some competitions, a half-pipe ramp isn't big enough. In these events, riders may do tricks off a MegaRamp. A MegaRamp is a giant half-pipe ramp. These huge ramps are most often used in snowboarding competitions, where it's known as a SuperPipe. However, they are becoming more and more common in BMX and skateboard competitions. Because the pipe is so much bigger, athletes are able to get bigger air and do never-before-seen tricks.

Rider Steve McCann pulls off a can can.

Can Can

The can can is a popular trick for BMX vert riders. While airborne, the rider kicks his or her leg over the bike. Then the rider puts the leg back before landing.

Aerial Spin

Aerial spins are some of the most important tricks in vert riding. To do a spin, the BMXer makes the entire bike spin while airborne. Aerial spins are measured in degrees such as 180, 360, 540, 720, and 900. One full circle is 360 degrees. In a 360, the rider uses the ramp to complete one full rotation. A 540 is one and a half spins. A 720 is two full spins.

Tailwhip

In a tailwhip, the rider whips the bike around the handlebars while airborne. Instead of standing on the pedals, the rider stays suspended

CHAD KAGY

Chad Kagy proved that he loved bikes from an early age. He was only eight years old when he entered his first BMX race. He turned pro at the age of 17. In 2003 he broke his neck, an injury that leaves many people paralyzed for life. But he competed at the 2004 X Games just nine months later. Kagy's amazing recovery earned him the nickname the Comeback Kid. When not competing, he travels to the Middle East to perform BMX shows for U.S. troops with a group called Bikes Over Baghdad.

above the bike, so the bike turns beneath the pro.

Flair

A flair is one of the most popular BMX vert tricks. The rider combines a backflip with a 180 spin. That way, the rider lands facing the right direction to speed up the other side of the ramp.

Chad Kagy does a flair.

WOODWARD

CHAPTER FOUR

BECOMING A CHAMPION

Most vert BMXers ride because they love the sport. They show off tricks for their friends and family. They practice new moves to challenge themselves. Still some riders dream of making it to the X Games. But a rider has to get noticed before participating in any of the big vert events.

Going Pro

With so many people participating in BMX vert, it can be tough for a rider to make it to the pros. Sponsors may discover some lucky riders while they are practicing in skate

Rider Austin Coleman does a tailwhip during the 2009 Dew Tour.

Pros don't spend all of their time competing. Wheels of Freestyle is a BMX group that performs at schools.

parks. Other pros create names for themselves by winning smaller competitions. Another way for riders to get recognized is by filming themselves doing tricks. A rider can then post videos of these tricks online for the world to see.

AUSTIN COLEMAN

Up-and-coming vert rider Austin Coleman started his action sports career as a skateboarder. After spraining his ankle, he borrowed his brother's BMX bike. Coleman went on to become a top BMX competitor. He is skilled at many styles of BMX biking. But he is best on vert's half-pipe ramp. He has been a regular Dew Tour competitor since 2006. In 2012 he made it to the X Games vert finals. He came in fifth with a final score of 64. Coleman is definitely a vert rider to watch.

Sponsors such as Red Bull help pros like Kevin Robinson ride professionally.

Most rookie riders know that going pro is a long shot. But if an amateur rider gets good enough, a brand may offer to sponsor that rider. Sponsors provide vert riders with equipment and money. Learning vert tricks takes a lot of time. Sponsored riders can make learning new tricks their full-time jobs. A sponsored rider makes money by doing commercials and competing. Red Bull, DC, Rockstar Energy Drink, and etnies are some major sponsors of BMX vert riders. Many of these brands also help sponsor competitions where pros from around the world can face off against one another.

Competitions

Competitions feature pros pushing the limits of vert riding. These pros pull off tricks that wow fans and judges alike. The competitions may look fun for the pros—and they are. But these professionals are true competitors who have a lot on the line.

WOMEN IN VERT

Women's vert is still a relatively new sport. The 2012 X Games did not feature any women's BMX events. A few BMX competitions feature women's events. But these events usually get less publicity. As a result, there are fewer sponsors for women. Female riders often have to pay their own transportation costs when they travel to BMX competitions. Several female riders are hoping to change this. BMX vert rider Natalie Wade and other female BMXers are trying to bring more attention to women's freestyle BMX. They hope that if there is more coverage of women riding, more girls will try the sport. More interest will mean more sponsors and maybe even a spot in the X Games. Right now it's not easy being a pro female rider, but that could soon change.

BMX riding doesn't have a regular season like basketball or baseball. But several major events throughout the year bring the top BMX vert riders together. Mountain Dew hosts its Dew Tour every year. The Dew Tour also has an amateur series. Rookie riders who win in the amateur series have a shot at making it to the pro tour. Red Bull also sponsors several BMX vert competitions throughout the year. For most riders and fans, the biggest vert competition of the year is ESPN's X Games.

Vert rider Jay Miron does a 540 at a Dew Tour competition.

25

Winning

In the X Games vert competition, each rider does a series of runs on the half-pipe ramp. In each run, the rider gets 30 seconds to do as many tricks as possible. Judges score each run out of 50 points. The score is based on both the tricks' levels of difficulty and how well the rider performs the tricks. In the 2012 X Games, each rider had the chance to do four runs. After the final run, a rider's two highest scores are combined to create his or her final score. Jamie Bestwick's final score in 2012 was 86 out of a possible 100 points.

Where to Watch

ESPN and ABC network broadcast the X Games BMX vert events every summer. After the games are over, fans can watch video highlights online.

Fans who don't want to wait until the X Games to watch vert stunts can ask a parent or another adult to help them find videos online. Every day pros and amateurs film themselves doing awesome tricks. Videos of these tricks are available on websites such as YouTube. But remember to only try tricks within your skill level. Trying to copy moves shown in online videos can be a quick way to get hurt!

It's important to start slow when learning a new BMX move. Riders should only try moves within their skill levels.

THE BREAKDOWN OF A BMX BIKE

WHEELS

The wheels on a BMX bike are much wider than regular bike wheels. Most pro vert riders use wheels 20 inches (51 centimeters) wide or wider. Skinnier wheels couldn't handle the stress of vert tricks.

GEARS

Most BMX bikes have a big gear in the front with 25 teeth. The teeth connect the big gear to a smaller gear (with nine teeth) on the back wheel. The gears and wheels are connected in a freewheel style. Freewheeling allows riders to pedal bikes backward without the bike stopping or changing directions.

CRANK

A crank connects the pedals to the gear.

HANDLEBARS

Most adult vert riders use lifted handlebars that measure 7.5 to 9 inches (19 to 23 cm) from the stem to the handlebar grip. This style of handlebars gives the rider more control while doing tricks. Vert bikes have a detangler rotor connected to the handlebars. The detangler rotor allows a vert rider to spin the handlebars all the way around without tangling up the brake cables if a rider is using a bike with brakes.

TOP TUBE

The top tube is the top piece of a bike frame. A rider's height decides how high from the ground the top tube should be.

PEGS

Pegs allow riders to do additional tricks such as grinds along the edge of the ramp. Most vert bikes have four pegs, two in the front and two in the back.

PEDALS

Most BMX vert riders use a platform pedal. A platform pedal is larger than those used on other types of bikes. Platform pedals give a rider's feet a lot of grip. This helps riders make tough landings without worrying about their feet slipping off.

GLOSSARY

AMATEUR

someone who participates in an activity for fun without expectation of payment

COMBOS

groups of tricks done together

HALF PIPE

a ramp used in extreme sports that looks like half the inside of a pipe

HEAT

a round of BMX runs that decides which competitors will advance to the finals

MAINSTREAM

something that is commonly accepted

PROFESSIONAL

someone who participates in an activity as a job for payment

QUARTER PIPE

a ramp used in extreme sports that looks like one-quarter of the inside of a pipe

ROOKIE

someone who is new to a sport or activity

RUN

a set of tricks

SPONSOR

a company that financially supports professional athletes in a sport so they can focus on that sport

FOR MORE INFORMATION

Books

Bishop, Amanda, and Bobbie Kalman. *Extreme BMX*. New York: Crabtree Publishing, 2004.

Cain, Patrick G. *BMX Street*. Minneapolis: Lerner Publications, 2013.

Thomas, Isabel. *Freestyle BMX*. Minneapolis: Lerner Publications, 2012.

Websites

ESPN X Games
http://espn.go.com/action/xgames
The official X Games website features information about the X Games. Check out BMX vert athlete bios, videos, and scores, and find out when and where the next X Games will be held.

Jamie Bestwick Bio
http://www.kidzworld.com/article/25155-jamie-bestwick-bio
Visit this website to learn more about famous BMX vert pro Jamie Bestwick.

Livestrong.com BMX
http://www.livestrong.com/bmx/
This website provides facts about BMX biking. It includes information on safety gear, BMX history, and more about the world of BMX biking.

INDEX

About the Author

Patrick Cain is a nuclear engineer turned writer. He is an award-winning journalist whose work often appears in a number of magazines such as *ESPN the Magazine* and *Fast Company*. He currently lives in Los Angeles, California, but will forever be tied to upstate New York.